A Christmas Heart

THE STORY OF MARY

A devotional

Unless otherwise noted, scripture quotations are from:
The Holy Bible, New International Version (NIV).
Zondervan, 1973, 1978, 1984, 2011.

Other scripture references are from the following sources:
The Message (MSG). NavPress Publishing Group, 1993.
The Passion Translation. Broadstreet Publishing Group, LLC, 2015.

Unless otherwise noted, all recipes are sourced from family members and published with their permission.
The Sugar Cookie recipe is from:
"The Best Sugar Cookies." Recipe. bhg.com.
N.p., n.d. Web. 23 November, 2020.

Edited by Ali Hooper; www.alihooper.com
Cover and interior design by Kreativity Inc.; www.kreativityinc.com

Table of Contents

Dedication

To the four wonderful mothers in my life.

To the all American Grandma, Dollie Godbey. She always made a farm Christmas so special with her homemade apple pie and brown paper bags of penny candy. Most of all, Christmas was always special because of her deep mothering love.

To Hazel Beatrice Bell, "Granny Hazel." She spoiled all 12 of us cousins with kisses that filled our cheeks. We filled her country kitchen as she filled us up with homemade everything from the garden, but most of all she filled the hearts of each and every one of us with unconditional love.

To my mother-n-love, Betty Jackson. You taught me numerous invaluable life lessons about prayer, Bible study and being a wife in full time ministry. You deposited in me an appreciation for cleaning, the art of Southern cooking and a passion for pretty things. I'm deeply grateful.

To my own beautiful mother, Sherrie Ellen Godbey. You bring me joy, and you have shared the Christmas heart of God with me all my life. You live a life worthy of Him in every way. We love all the same things such as books, writing, flowers, makeup, china dishes, cooking, shopping, worship songs and so much more! I love you, Mom.

Introduction

A CHRISTMAS HEART
The Story of Mary

I don't know about you, but for me, Christmastime is a season full of mixed emotions. There is joy and good will, but there is also pain, grief and heartache. Often we make Christmas about the things of Christmas - the presents, the parties and the picture-perfect photo, adding to the weight of the season. But what if Christmas was actually an opportunity to transform your heart and experience the greatest gift of all? What if, by adopting a Christmas heart, we experienced the highs and lows of the season with deeper faith, richer experiences and greater praise? It's possible. It's possible because your access to a Christmas heart is as simple as connecting with what is already right there: Emmanuel, God with us.

A Christmas heart is not a heart that puts on a happy face and throws more tinsel at the season. Rather a Christmas heart is a heart that longs for Jesus. A Christmas heart finds joy in relationship with Jesus through prayer, worship and praise. A Christmas heart holds tightly to Jesus, our Emmanuel, God with us. He is at the center of everything in our lives.

As the Christmas season unfolds, I dream that you will take time to soak in the scriptures about Mary and Jesus. Don't rush through them, but rather simmer on the Christmas word of God like mulled cider on the stove top. Take time to sit, slow down and enjoy His presence which in turn will bring you great comfort and hope. Christmas is a time of reflection into the heart of the season. My desire is to share a Christmas heart with you by taking a deeper look at the Christmas story through the lens of God's word. You can read through this devotional a week at a time, saving the final chapter for Christmas Day, or travel at your own pace. Maybe you gather friends to take this journey with you, discussing the scriptures and questions together for richer study. There are no rules. It's your journey to savor.

Each chapter begins with a quick sentence prayer in the hopes of grounding your spirit before you dig into the content. The chapters end with practical steps for application that first include a verse from scripture for memorization, and I encourage you to pray each scripture over your own life. The *Words Worth Repeating* sections provide statements and themes that are easy to remember. The reflection questions are great journal prompts or discussion points for you to engage in your time with God or with friends. The prayers at the end of each chapter are prayers that I've prayed over my own life, and I pray them also for you. I hope you'll join me in these prayers. Finally, each chapter closes with a favorite holiday recipe that I've enjoyed with my own family, and I hope you will enjoy with yours. Through this devotional, may Mary come alive as you implement the lessons she teaches. May your life mirror hers, and may your heart soften to Jesus. I pray that you discover Emmanuel through this journey. God was with Mary. He is with me, and He is with you. Living inside of our hearts and guiding us with His Spirit, He is our peace, our hope and our salvation.

This Christmas, may your heart be transformed to reflect Emmanuel: God with us.

Do you believe?

START WITH A QUICK
SENTENCE PRAYER

———————

Jesus, I treasure you.

Chapter 1

MARY TREASURED AND PONDERED

My son Aaron's due date was December 27th. For nine months I anticipated a Christmas baby and the joy that would be delivered during an already joy-filled time of year. As the holiday season ramped up, I prepared myself for his arrival. My hospital bag was packed, my Christmas cards were mailed, and the house was decorated. That year we invited family and friends to join us for a Christmas light display and walking tour. While walking, I realized that I was beginning to have contractions, though they were mild. Because my heart was happy and full and because the contractions were not yet significant, I kept going, enjoying the beautiful lights and the wonderful company. With the buttons on my maternity winter coat ready to pop, I breathed in the hope of Christmas air through my red scarf as I merrily waddled along. Nevertheless, the unexpected soon became a reality as my son Aaron decided to arrive nearly two weeks early.

BUT MARY TREASURED UP ALL THESE THINGS AND PONDERED THEM IN HER HEART. *Luke 2:19*

FOR WHERE YOUR TREASURE IS, THERE YOUR HEART WILL BE ALSO. *Matthew 6:21*

On December 16th, 1992, my husband and I were together in a hospital room, surrounded by doctors and nurses, as I delivered our 6 pound 1 ounce baby boy. By the grace of God, I might add! We discovered the cord was in a knot, wrapped around his neck, and Aaron's early delivery was truly the mercy of God.

Though we were expecting him, Aaron's arrival took us by surprise. I have never been so excited in my entire life as I was bringing home that tiny baby just days before Christmas. I dressed him in a cute red and green outfit and placed him under our tree for a photo-op. He was the best gift ever.

Though it's been many years since I squeezed into that maternity coat, the memory of that night remains fresh in my mind, and each December I relive the joy of celebrating our son's birthday just days before we celebrate the birth of another son - Mary's son, Jesus.

WHEN WE LONG TO ENCOUNTER JESUS AND ANTICIPATE HIS PRESENCE IN OUR LIVES, WE HAVE A CHRISTMAS HEART.

I just love Mother Mary. She truly had a Christmas heart. She knew what it was like to carry Jesus inside her womb, to love someone before ever seeing his face, to anticipate his arrival and to long to meet him at delivery. Like Mary, we too can carry Jesus inside of us and have a Christmas heart. A Christmas heart is a heart that loves the Messiah. When we long to encounter Jesus and anticipate His presence in our lives, we have a Christmas heart. That transformative relationship with Jesus is central to the Christmas story that we celebrate in December every year.

Scripture tells us that after Mary gave birth to Jesus, angels appeared to shepherds nearby. The angels told the shepherds of the good news: the Messiah was born. When the shepherds saw that it was true, they spread the good news, and "all who heard it were amazed at what the shepherds said to them. But Mary treasured up all these things and pondered them in her heart" (Luke 2:19).

Things flee quickly but Treasures last a lifetime.

Mary treasured, and she pondered. For me, the words treasure and ponder mean to slow down, reflect, remember and preserve. Mary did just that with the good news that she had delivered so humbly in a manger. As she held baby Jesus, she reflected on who He would be to the world, and she preserved all that in her heart and soul.

Mary was sentimental, and she was one to think deeply. So much of the Christmas season can be hectic and busy. In fact, so much of life can be hectic and busy. But Mary reflected on what mattered most, such as God and her family. She was aware of God's good, perfect and pleasing will, and she treasured His gifts in her heart. It's easy for us to get wrapped up in the tangible things of Christmas like the presents, the food and the activities, but a Christmas heart is a heart that cherishes Jesus. Things flee quickly but treasures last a lifetime.

Mary also treasured her nation, Israel. In Luke 1, she sang a prayerful song that reflected God's goodness to His people: the descendants of Abraham for generations. When baby Jesus arrived and the shepherds spread the good news of His arrival, Mary's heart contemplated the good news that would save God's people for generations.

I can relate to Mary. As a mother, I like to remember and reflect, keeping boxes of kids' school papers and art projects as special treasures for safekeeping. My youngest son, Peter, crafts hand-blown glass ornaments, and these creations are precious to me. Maybe you have items that have been given or passed down to you that you treasure. Many of us hang special ornaments on our Christmas trees that are treasures or gifts from our past.

We also reflect on memories. I used to have a dear friend named Louise who lost her life to Leukemia. When my son Aaron was only days old, Louise gave me silver cookie cutters as a Christmas gift. At the time, Louise was in the final stages of her battle against the disease. She said to me, "I want you to promise me that every year you will remember me when you make and decorate cookies with your boys." She went on to say that the time I spent together with my boys making cookies was as important as any gift under the tree. Her gift of cookie cutters and the keeping of that promise has gifted my family with years of joy-filled baking. Those memories are sealed in my mind forever, and Louise remains a special part of our Christmas season as we bake and remember her.

Traditions allow us to cherish and reflect. The Christmas season is also a time that lends itself to thinking about all of the goodness that God has displayed in our lives throughout the year. When we look back, we discover His miracles at work in our lives through restored relationships, forgiveness offered and received and the freedom that comes through a life with Jesus.

By slowing down, pausing and pondering, we can see the bigger picture of how God has moved around us and throughout the world in so many special ways.

God meets us through people, places and His presence.

What a gift to reflect on just that - people, places and the presence of Jesus. It's easy to be weighed down by difficult circumstances, relationships and hardships, but Mary is a beautiful reminder that we can find joy when we think, treasure and ponder Jesus. He summed it up beautifully Himself in Matthew 6:21 when He said, "For where your treasure is, there your heart will be also." Jesus really is the reason for the season.

We all need some good news to hold onto during the holiday season. We have the arrival of a Savior, one who saves us both for eternity and for the hope, joy and peace we so desperately long for at Christmas and always. That's good news! But what happens after you receive the good news? What can we do with a Christmas heart, a heart that treasures Jesus? Mary shows us that God has much in store for us when we live a life centered around Jesus. Does God have much in store for you? Could God, who called Mary to mother baby Jesus, also call you to something extraordinary? I believe He already has.

This year, when you open up the tin of cookie cutters and as you make Christmas-shaped cookies with your loved ones, think about Jesus. Talk about Him with your family and friends as you indulge in traditions together. Talk about what you treasure. Reflect on the tiny miracles of life all around you. Ponder God's goodness. Cultivate a Christmas heart like Mary's, and savor this special month of treasuring and pondering as you receive the greatest gift of all, Jesus.

Now that you have the greatest treasure of all, are you ready for what's next?

LUKE 2:15-19

WHEN THE ANGELS HAD LEFT THEM AND
GONE INTO HEAVEN, THE SHEPHERDS
SAID TO ONE ANOTHER, "LET'S GO TO
BETHLEHEM AND SEE THIS THING THAT
HAS HAPPENED, WHICH THE LORD HAS
TOLD US ABOUT." SO THEY HURRIED OFF
AND FOUND MARY AND JOSEPH, AND THE
BABY, WHO WAS LYING IN THE MANGER.
WHEN THEY HAD SEEN HIM, THEY SPREAD
THE WORD CONCERNING WHAT HAD BEEN
TOLD THEM ABOUT THIS CHILD, AND ALL
WHO HEARD IT WERE AMAZED AT WHAT
THE SHEPHERDS SAID TO THEM. BUT MARY
TREASURED UP ALL THESE THINGS AND
PONDERED THEM IN HER HEART.

PRAYER

Dear Jesus, I treasure you.
Your birth was so much more
than a story we remember at
Christmastime. Rather, your
arrival delivered hope, promise
and salvation for generations, and
I treasure these gifts in my heart.
When I ponder your presence in
my life, I am met with your warm
embrace, your sacrificial love and
your constant goodness. My heart
and soul are transformed because
of you. Thank you for living and
dying for me. Jesus, I treasure
you. Amen.

MEMORIZE

But Mary treasured all these things and pondered them in her heart.

Luke 2:19

words worth repeating

A CHRISTMAS HEART IS A HEART
THAT CHERISHES JESUS.

THINGS FLEE QUICKLY BUT
TREASURES LAST A LIFETIME.

DISCOVER HIS MIRACLES
THROUGH RESTORED
RELATIONSHIPS, FORGIVENESS
OFFERED AND RECEIVED AND THE
FREEDOM THAT COMES THROUGH
A LIFE WITH JESUS.

TODAY I PONDER PEOPLE, PLACES
AND THE PRESENCE OF JESUS.

JESUS, I TREASURE YOU.

REFLECTION

*What is the best gift you
have ever received?*

*What do you treasure?
What do you treasure most?*

*On what do you reflect,
ponder or contemplate?*

*Reflect on the tiny miracles
of life in the world around
you. What do they mean
to you?*

*What are you grateful for
this Christmas season?*

*How can you incorporate
time to "ponder and
treasure" the things of
God?*

*Have you received the
greatest gift, the gift of
Jesus?*

Better Homes
and Gardens:
Blaine Moats

INGREDIENTS

2/3 cup butter, softened
3/4 cup sugar
1 teaspoon baking powder
1/4 teaspoon salt
1 egg
1 tablespoon milk
1 teaspoon vanilla
2 cups all-purpose flour

My favorite sugar
cookie recipe!
From Better Homes & Gardens

DIRECTIONS

In a large bowl beat butter on medium to high speed for 30 seconds. Add sugar, baking powder, and salt. Beat until combined, scraping sides of bowl occasionally. Beat in egg, milk, and vanilla until combined. Beat in as much of the flour as you can with the mixer. Using a wooden spoon, stir in any remaining flour. Divide dough in half. Cover; chill about 30 minutes or until dough is easy to handle.

Preheat oven to 375°F. On a lightly floured surface, roll dough, half at a time, until 1/8 to 1/4 inch thick. Using 2-1/2-inch cookie cutters, cut dough into desired shapes. Place cutouts 1 inch apart on ungreased cookie sheets. Repeat with the remaining dough.

Bake for about 7 minutes or until the edges are very light brown. Transfer to wire racks; cool. If desired, frost with your favorite icing and/or decorate with decorative candies.

START WITH A QUICK
SENTENCE PRAYER

*Jesus, I am available
and willing.*

Chapter 2

MARY WAS AVAILABLE, WILLING & CALLED

When I was a young girl, only 20 years old, God called me to live in Israel. That season of my life was indescribable, and one of the greatest highlights of my experience (and possibly one of the greatest highlights of my life) was Christmastime in the town of Bethlehem.

> I AM THE LORD'S SERVANT. MAY YOUR WORD TO ME BE FULFILLED.
>
> *Luke 1:38*

For many weeks I rehearsed Christmas songs with other believers of many different backgrounds and nationalities as we prepared for a Christmas celebration in Bethlehem. Our rehearsals took place inside a magnificent church within the old city walls of Jerusalem. The acoustics of the church were phenomenal, and the rehearsals themselves were a glimpse into eternity. Our performance would take place in Bethlehem, and our audience would be people from countries all over the world who were traveling to be as close as possible to where the Christmas story all began.

Christmas Eve finally arrived, and I was on a bus with the other performers to the town of Bethlehem. I was wearing a red Christmas dress with a white lace collar, a handmade gift from my mother. As I sat there missing my family and my mother's delicious stuffing, I reflected on the significance of mothers and grandmothers, both my own and Mother Mary. I was reminded of the great value of motherhood and the profound call on a mother's life, especially the call on Mother Mary's life. As we approached Bethlehem, I could see beautiful rolling hills with shepherds in their flowing headdresses and sheep grazing the pasture. It was as if time had stood still since Christ's birth hundreds of years ago. We passed the Church of the Nativity, and soon approached Manger Square. The sun had nearly set, and I could see the crowds that had gathered to hear us sing. The sky turned the color of deep sapphire blue, and the stars were twinkling brightly. There I stood in my handmade Christmas dress overlooking this tiny town of God-hungry travelers. Together we humbly worshipped on holy ground as we sang *O Holy Night*. It had been 2000 years since Christ was born at nearly that exact location, and there we sang with the shepherd's fields as our backdrop and the starry hosts in the sky. I could feel Heaven join in our singing, *Glory to God and Peace on Earth*.

When God called me to Israel, I never imagined I would take part in such a transformative experience. That year changed me, imprinting on my heart a deep longing to experience more of Jesus everyday. However, when God first called me to Israel, I faced doubts, fears and questions. I would be leaving the comforts of the life I had always known, comforts that included a supportive family, a network of friends and mocha lattes. Not to mention, I had to replace my favorite dresses and shoes for hiking boots and jeans. That was a hard adjustment for a Southern girl in the 1980s!

In Scripture we read about Mary, the mother of Jesus, and we read about the extraordinary journey that God had for her. The call on her life would put her very life at risk, not simply because she would be pregnant, but also because it implied an adulterous relationship (Joseph knew he was not the father). Adultery was criminally scandalous at that time in history.

Prior to the call on her life, Mary lived a simple life. She was a young, humble and lowly girl. She was ordinary.

THERE WAS NOTHING IN MARY'S LIFE THAT POINTED TO THE EXTAORDINARY CALL THAT WOULD BE PLACED ON HER LIFE.

"God sent the angel Gabriel to Nazareth, a town in Galilee, to a virgin pledged to be married to a man named Joseph, a descendant of David. The virgin's name was Mary. The angel went to her and said, Greetings, you who are highly favored! The Lord is with you" (Luke 1:26-28).

The angel gave Mary an assignment that was so much bigger than her situation. Gabriel said to her, "You will conceive and give birth to a son, and you are to call him Jesus. He will be great and will be called the Son of the Most High" (Luke 1:31-32). Mary responded with a question of how, clarifying to the angel, "I am a virgin" (Luke 1:34). Doesn't that sound like you and me? When God calls us, we often respond with the words, "how" and "but." Nonetheless, God was gracious to Mary, offering her an explanation. The angel told Mary that the Holy Spirit would come upon her, and her child would be the Son of God.

What I love about Mary is that she was fully aware, in tune, listening and almost unknowingly ready for this task. I wonder about Mary: did she pray while she cleaned, did she enjoy school when she studied the Hebrew scriptures or did she sing to God in the fields? I wonder how much Mary was like most of us when we were young. Did she talk back to her parents? Did she roll her eyes at every little thing her mom suggested? Did she keep a diary hidden under her mattress? Likely she was both a young girl who sighed loudly when asked to clean the house and a maturing lady who God was preparing for this moment in time.

A Christmas heart is a heart available to God's plans. Are you available and willing or busy and uninterested? When we invest our days in Him, our hearts soften toward His instructions to us and His plans for us. Mary's fear didn't keep her from the quick response of Yes to God that would follow the angel's message to her. Additionally, scripture tells us that God favored Mary simply because He favored her. It was not because of anything that she did (or didn't do) or said (or didn't

A CHRISTMAS HEART IS A HEART AVAILABLE TO GOD'S PLANS. ARE YOU AVAILABL AND WILLING OR BUSY AND UNINTERESTE say) that made God favor her. Rather, it was the grace of God that called Mary to mother the Son of God.

No matter the season, God meets you right where you are. If you are in a season of laundry, dishes and diapers, God is there. If you are in a season of mounting job stress, God is there. If you are in a season of teenage angst, God is there. If you are in a season of loss and mourning, God is there. No matter your season, God is with you as you move through it. A Christmas heart is a heart that recognizes God is with you despite the chaos around you.

A Christmas hearts is a heart that recognizes God is with you despite the chaos around you.

Just as Mary was highly favored and called, you also are highly favored and called by God. He has a specific assignment for you to fulfill. He has a purpose for your life, not because of anything you have done but because He longs to be gracious to you. Nothing can hold you back from His best plans for your life - not your fear, not your sin, not your emotions, not your past. Not a single thing in your life is bigger than God's grace in your life. That grace allows you to pray with confidence: "Lord, don't let me waste my life."

Mary was a young woman when God invited her to an enormous task, yet before He called her, He encouraged her. The angel's first words to her were, "You are highly favored! The Lord is with you" (Luke 1:28). Let me assure you, God favors you too. "The Lord longs to be gracious to you; therefore he will rise up to show you compassion" (Isaiah 30:18). Different translations use different words to capture God's quickness in showing us His grace - words including mercy, faithfulness, love and blessing. God does not see His children and rank them in order of how much He respects them so that He can bless them accordingly. Rather, God sees His children through His heart of grace, mercy, love and promise. The Lord favors you just like He did Mary.

The Lord favors you just like He did Mary.

Without hesitation, Mary displayed the beauty of willingness. Her Christmas heart was a heart that was available to God for His plans. Mary was a virgin; she was committed to purity. Scripture does not say that God favored Mary because she was a virgin. However, her purity allowed her to be available to this call on her life. She had simply surrendered, and the result was sweet success.

She responded to the angel, saying, "I am the Lord's servant. May your word to me be fulfilled" (Luke 1:38). The Passion Translation reads, "This is amazing! I will be a mother for the Lord! As his servant, I accept whatever he has for me. May everything you have told me come to pass." In other words, Mary surrendered everything to God's plan. Surrender is simply being satisfied with God's story for you. Mary knew that God's plan was for her to carry this baby inside her womb, and she knew this plan would reach the public. There would be no way to hide her faith as her belly grew. Even so, she surrendered her body, her womb, her reputation, her plans and her emotions. Mary was all in for Jesus. Mary had a living faith, and that living faith is accessible to us as well.

What if you lived in such a way that you were not afraid to be all in for Jesus? What would it look like for you to say Yes to God despite your fear, your past, your sin and your circumstances? What would it look like for you to surrender everything to Him, even the emotions that are holding you back?

Several years ago as I was recovering from a surgery, I walked and prayed the streets near our home as a way to progress my recovery. I asked the Lord about my future, and He spoke clearly and directly to me. He gave me two directives: 1) Say yes to Doyle (my husband) and 2) Say yes to Columbus. I responded, "OK, God, yes, of course I will," and then I thought, "Wait a minute. I thought I was already doing those things."

God gently opened my eyes to see new ways in which I could change my heart and attitude. Though I had said yes to Doyle and Columbus, within that yes there were reservations and conditional statements. God helped me to see the many ways in which I could shift my heart to better help, love and serve my family and our city. Tears began to flow down my cheeks as my heart replied, *Yes, Lord.* I committed to spending more time praying for Doyle and the boys, living more generously and less tight-fisted with my schedule and shifting my energy toward developing leaders and helping our church. A weight lifted as I said yes to the Lord, and a new joy filled my heart.

When I surrendered it all to God that day, I gained a fresh and heavenly love for both my husband and the city where we serve. I was overwhelmed by God's detailed instructions and the depth of motivation I felt to follow Him with those two clear assignments. I can now see how God has used us to reach others for Him, and it all started with that surrender: Yes to God, Yes to family and Yes to our city. I can say confidently: It's all been worth it.

What incredible gifts might God have in store for us when we say Yes to Him? What might it look like this Christmas for us to live with a Christmas heart - a heart that is available and willing to God's call on our lives? Mary surrendered to God which made way for a sweet success in her story. She said Yes to Emmanuel. Emmanuel means God with us. Mary's Christmas heart was transformed by Emmanuel - quite literally! We too have the opportunity to be transformed by Emmanual when we surrender to God's story for our lives. What sweetness might God deliver to us through Jesus when we say Yes to the story that He is writing for our lives?

Maybe you are thinking, "Yes, I'm willing and available, but I am suffering. The pain is too much." God knows what you are suffering, and Mary knew suffering too. She offers us a precious example of a Christmas heart that seeks Jesus even in the thick of deep sorrow.

> Will you join her in discovering God in the darkness?

LUKE 1:28-38

THE ANGEL WENT TO HER AND SAID, "GREETINGS, YOU WHO ARE HIGHLY FAVORED! THE LORD IS WITH YOU." MARY WAS GREATLY TROUBLED AT HIS WORDS AND WONDERED WHAT KIND OF GREETING THIS MIGHT BE. BUT THE ANGEL SAID TO HER, "DO NOT BE AFRAID, MARY; YOU HAVE FOUND FAVOR WITH GOD. YOU WILL CONCEIVE AND GIVE BIRTH TO A SON, AND YOU ARE TO CALL HIM JESUS. HE WILL BE GREAT AND WILL BE CALLED THE SON OF THE MOST HIGH. THE LORD GOD WILL GIVE HIM THE THRONE OF HIS FATHER DAVID, AND HE WILL REIGN OVER JACOB'S DESCENDANTS FOREVER; HIS KINGDOM WILL NEVER END."

"HOW WILL THIS BE," MARY ASKED THE ANGEL, "SINCE I AM A VIRGIN?"

THE ANGEL ANSWERED, "THE HOLY SPIRIT WILL COME ON YOU, AND THE POWER OF THE MOST HIGH WILL OVERSHADOW YOU. SO THE HOLY ONE TO BE BORN WILL BE CALLED THE SON OF GOD. EVEN ELIZABETH YOUR RELATIVE IS GOING TO HAVE A CHILD IN HER OLD AGE, AND SHE WHO WAS SAID TO BE UNABLE TO CONCEIVE IS IN HER SIXTH MONTH. FOR NO WORD FROM GOD WILL EVER FAIL."

"I AM THE LORD'S SERVANT," MARY ANSWERED. "MAY YOUR WORD TO ME BE FULFILLED." THEN THE ANGEL LEFT HER.

PRAYER

Dear God, I humbly bow my
head before you, my holy God.
Help me to be like Mary and
listen for your directions. I choose
to say Yes to you and No to
fear and anxiety. Don't let me
waste my life. Give me peace as
the details of your plans for me
unfold. I am willing to step out in
faith to follow you; I'm available
for any assignment. Speak Lord,
my ears and heart are open now. I
want to fulfill all of the plans and
purposes you have for my life.
Amen.

Pray this scripture over your own life:
I am the Lord's servant. May your word to me be fulfilled.

"I am the Lord's servant," Mary answered. "May your word to me be fulfilled." Then the angel left her.

Luke 1:38

words worth repeating

AM I AVAILABLE AND WILLING OR
BUSY AND UNINTERESTED?

NOT A SINGLE THING IN YOUR LIFE IS
BIGGER THAN GOD'S GRACE IN YOUR LIFE.

I AM HIGHLY FAVORED AND CALLED.

SIMPLY SURRENDER FOR SWEET SUCCESS.

SURRENDER IS SIMPLY BEING SATISFIED
WITH GOD'S STORY FOR ME.

REFLECTION

What has God called you to that is bigger than what you deemed possible?

Are there any limits you have put on your life by believing a lie? What lies?

What is God calling you to this week?

When God calls you to something, what feelings do you experience?

What excuses have you made to get out of God's call on your life?

How could you surrender your emotions to God this week in order to say yes to Him?

How has God blessed you unexpectedly through your willingness to say yes to Him? Reflect on the past, and ponder a time in your life when you said yes to God's instructions. What about that experience do you still treasure today?

MOM'S STUFFING

Hi Jenny,

I can't find a written recipe, but this is what I do:

I make a pan of cornbread, using the recipe on the bag of self-rising cornmeal. This can be made ahead of time and kept in the refrigerator for a few days.

I add a bag of Pepperidge Farm mixed bread stuffing mix to the crumbled cornbread.

I cook/scramble a pound of mild sausage and add it to the bread mixture.

I saute one big onion and some stalks of celery, diced, in a stick of butter and add it to the bread mixture (including the butter).

I mix a lot of fresh sage (or a can of sage) to the bread mixture (maybe a whole small can).

I beat a couple of eggs into a can of chicken broth and add it to the bread mixture. I then add more chicken broth if needed. You can make the dressing as moist or dry as you want.

I would probably taste the dressing to see if it needs pepper or salt (probably not).

I like to put some stuffing inside the turkey, and I use the recipe on the turkey roasting bag to bake the turkey. It tells you the time to bake it and what to do to the roasting bag.

If you use a pan to bake the stuffing, you will need to grease the pan with butter or shortening or it will really stick to the pan.

I can't think of anything else that I do. I did find a recipe that I had on an old computer disk. It calls for turkey giblets, which I have used, but that's not necessary. Mom always cooked the neck, etc. and removed the meat from the bones, chopped it and added it to the dressing. Sometimes I do; sometimes I don't.

Lots of love,
Mom

START WITH A QUICK
SENTENCE PRAYER

*Jesus, meet me in
my suffering.*

Chapter 3

MARY WAS WOUNDED AND DISGRACED

I looked down at my hands as I wrapped a gift. "How can they look just like Allison's?" I closed my eyes, and my memory took me back to the front porch of a tiny two bedroom farm house in Eubank, Kentucky, surrounded by hills, cows, a creek and a tobacco barn. I hear the car pull into the driveway, and I run, determined to be the first one to reach my cousin. She opens the door, and together we race down the steps to the musty basement, laughing and squealing with joy. The memories begin to come faster. I remember sitting together under the glow of bubble lights strung around the tree. I remember our matching ladybug purses. I remember devouring Aunt Carolyn's brownies. I remember our late night laughter over the horrible smell of Grandma's bath powder.

> MARY WAS GREATLY TROUBLED AT HIS WORDS AND WONDERED WHAT KIND OF GREETING THIS MIGHT BE.
>
> *Luke 1:29*

My memory fast forwards to 20 years later, and we are together at a hotel near Vanderbilt Hospital where Allison is being tested to receive a possible treatment for her aggressive melanoma cancer. She suggests we go to the hotel hot tub, but I tell her that I don't have a bathing suit. She suggests we wear our Spanx, and so that we did. There in the hot tub, in all our glory and squeezed into our Spanx, we laughed and we laughed and we laughed. With Allison, there was always laughter. Now, our together laughter is only a memory. She left this earth on Christmas Day when she was much too young to die. I lost my dear friend and best cousin, and I lost new opportunities to laugh with her.

All of us who walk this dusty earth are wounded in some way or another; unfortunately there are no exemptions. Christmas can be a bittersweet time for many people. I know many who have lost loved ones, suffer deep family strife, endure the pain of wayward children or experience the holidays in isolation and loneliness. God does not take those wounds lightly. In the midst of all of our grief, pain and suffering, God invites us to draw close to Him and experience His caring comfort. Mary knew suffering and pain, and God cared for her.

And He cares deeply for you.

Jesus said that if we are to be His disciples, we must deny ourselves, take up His cross and follow Him (Luke 9:23). Mary certainly did this with a willing Christmas heart. We know that when God called her to be the mother of His Son, that didn't necessarily mean that society would accept her and God's plan for her. When the angel visited Mary to share with her the call on her life, scripture tells us that initially Mary was greatly troubled by the angel's visit (Luke 1:29).

Though Mary was pledged to marry Joseph, she was pregnant and a virgin. Joseph knew that he was not the father, and Joseph contemplated divorce. I wonder how this impacted their relationship. I wonder if she could feel him pulling away from her?

"Because Joseph her husband was faithful to the law, and yet did not want to expose her to public disgrace, he had in mind to divorce her quietly" (Matthew 1:19).

Had Joseph decided to make Mary's pregnancy public, Mary would have faced a terrible outcome. At that time in history, adultery was punishable, likely by death.

I think of Mary's unplanned pregnancy, and I wish we had the detailed version of all the conversations, gossip and family turmoil it brought into light. Can you imagine the conversations with his parents, her parents, his friends and her friends? Who else knew about this? We also know that after Joseph decided to stay with the engagement, Mary went to live with her cousin, Elizabeth, for three months. Did her family send her away? Was the time with Elizabeth an opportunity to let all the chatter die down? Think of all the accusations, lies and slander she likely faced.

We don't know all of the details, but we can be sure that no matter Mary's willingness, the circumstances caused her pain. By the grace of God, Joseph decided to stay with Mary, and together they were a power couple for the kingdom of God. He led Mary with godly leadership as he was led by God in dreams and through prayer. Together they moved through this journey, sharing in the pain, suffering and hardship.

Mary and Joseph were striving to be ideal new parents, so they worked hard to follow God's standards for families by being diligent and consistent parents. They went to Passover every year and celebrated many feasts, and when baby Jesus was only eight days old, they brought Him to the temple to be dedicated to God. Can you imagine being Mary? She had been through the trauma of birth in a stable, and a few short days later she traveled with her baby to the temple in Jerusalem.

Her trip to the temple reminds me of my friend, Layla, whom I met in Bethlehem. My husband and I hiked to Layla's house for a late lunch. With the sun beating down and the heat intensifying, I looked around at the green rocky hills dotted with sheep, goats and shepherds. I was awestruck as I thought, "Jesus is known across the entire world, and yet He was born in such a humble place." We reached Layla's small and simple home, and she greeted us with a tray of dates, figs, olives and stuffed grape leaves. I'll never forget the view from her kitchen window. The shepherds were holding large staffs as they herded the animals across the landscape. Layla said, "Everyday I look out this window in expectation just as the shepherds of old, but this time in expectation of Jesus' return. In my heart I pray, I am ready, Lord, I want to see you! I am looking forward to your return! Come again soon." Layla's Christmas heart longed for Jesus.

I imagine Layla still looks out her window, waiting for Jesus to come again. I imagine that Mary also longed for Jesus. After Jesus arrived, so many longed to encounter Him. Scripture tells us that the prophet, Simeon, waited expectedly in the temple for the Messiah.

Excited for the dedication of her baby, Mary and Joseph were met with a troubling prophecy that likely rocked their world that day at the temple. Simeon, who was at the temple, said, "This child is destined to cause the falling and rising of many in Israel, and to be a sign that will be spoken against, so that the thoughts of many hearts will be revealed. And a sword will pierce your own soul too" (Luke 2:34-35).

The Passion translation offers these words:

"A PAINFUL SWORD, MARY, WILL ONE DAY PIERCE YOUR INNER BEING, FOR YOUR CHILD WILL BE REJECTED BY MANY IN ISRAEL. AND THE DESTINY OF YOUR CHILD IS THIS: HE WILL BE LAID DOWN AS A MIRACLE SIGN FOR THE DOWNFALL AND RESURRECTION OF MANY IN ISRAEL. MANY WILL OPPOSE THIS SIGN, BUT IT WILL EXPOSE TO ALL THE INNERMOST THOUGHTS OF THEIR HEARTS BEFORE GOD."

Mary was no stranger to pain. Her heart was pierced at the thought of raising a child for such a destiny. Ponder this: Mary was alive and active during Jesus' ministry, His arrest and His trial, and then she was present at the foot of the cross when He was crucified. She saw the exciting fulfillment of God's plan, but she also endured a mother's trauma and anguish as she watched her son die a brutal, public death. We can only imagine how she was ultimately wounded by the pain of losing Jesus. There she was, huddled in the arms of her best friends at the foot of the cross and refusing to leave. She watched every devastating detail of her son's death. She didn't know He would later rise. At Jesus' crucifixion she only knew of His suffering. That was her baby, her son and her savior. Her heart spilled over as Jesus spoke to John, asking him to take care of His mother. The grief Mary must have felt when she couldn't see her son anymore.

In the middle of this pain-filled whirlwind, Emmanuel, God with us, provided a source of comfort for Mary in offering John's care. It wasn't the same as having Jesus Himself but it was a good provision nonetheless. God will also do that for you today right in the midst of your pain. He will speak, provide, heal and lead you.

The provisions for your life from the cross are endless.

"While the soldiers were looking after themselves, Jesus' mother, his aunt, Mary the wife of Clopas, and Mary Magdalene stood at the foot of the cross. Jesus saw his mother and the disciple he loved standing near her. He said to his mother, "Woman, here is your son." Then to the disciple, "Here is your mother." From that moment the disciple accepted her as his own mother" (John 19:26-27, The Message).

I don't know what hurts you today. I don't know the depth of your pain or the level of your struggle. But I do know this: you are still here. God is also still here. He sees your heart and every tear, and He cares and comforts, even today. I have several friends who have lost a child or miscarried, and I know that they understand this part of Mary's heart better than I do. They know the agony of anticipating the death of a child, and they know the heartbreaking reality of burying their baby.

From the moment she was with child to the foot of the cross, Mary demonstrated a Christmas heart. She remained wholly focused on Jesus in the midst of her pain, suffering and disgrace. She held the hope through the hard. A Christmas heart is crushed yet committed, damaged yet devoted. Because of Jesus, we can hold both our pain and the promise of hope. Jesus was pierced to provide our pierced hearts with purpose.

To develop a Christmas heart means to listen to the Simeon voices in our life. The prophet Simeon foresaw the suffering that Mary would endure, and he prophesied this eventual reality only one week after Jesus' birth. When we listen to the Simeon voices in our lives, we begin to realize that we will all be pierced. Suffering is an universal experience, but are you willing to follow your

God calling anyway? Are you willing to follow Jesus in those heart pierced moments and say, I trust you God? Can you lean in and say today, "I trust You God, even when it hurts." Mary placed Jesus' agenda above her own, and she embodied a Christmas heart focused on God's presence. God sent His son, Jesus - Emmanuel, to be with Mary, and He sent His son, Jesus - Emmanuel, to be God with us this Christmas.

Maybe you have experienced the presence of Jesus but still can't find the words to pray in the midst of your pain. By God's grace, Mary leads us in prayer and praise amidst her suffering.

Will you dare to offer hope through praise like Mary did?

LUKE 2:25, 27-35

———

NOW THERE WAS A MAN IN JERUSALEM CALLED
SIMEON, WHO WAS RIGHTEOUS AND DEVOUT. MOVED
BY THE SPIRIT, HE WENT INTO THE TEMPLE COURTS.
WHEN THE PARENTS BROUGHT IN THE CHILD JESUS
TO DO FOR HIM WHAT THE CUSTOM OF THE LAW
REQUIRED, SIMEON TOOK HIM IN HIS ARMS AND
PRAISED GOD, SAYING: "SOVEREIGN LORD, AS YOU
HAVE PROMISED, YOU MAY NOW DISMISS YOUR
SERVANT IN PEACE. FOR MY EYES HAVE SEEN YOUR
SALVATION, WHICH YOU HAVE PREPARED IN THE SIGHT
OF ALL NATIONS: A LIGHT FOR REVELATION TO THE
GENTILES, AND THE GLORY OF YOUR PEOPLE ISRAEL."
THE CHILD'S FATHER AND MOTHER MARVELED AT
WHAT WAS SAID ABOUT HIM. THEN SIMEON BLESSED
THEM AND SAID TO MARY, HIS MOTHER: "THIS CHILD
IS DESTINED TO CAUSE THE FALLING AND RISING
OF MANY IN ISRAEL, AND TO BE A SIGN THAT WILL
BE SPOKEN AGAINST, SO THAT THE THOUGHTS OF
MANY HEARTS WILL BE REVEALED. AND A SWORD WILL
PIERCE YOUR OWN SOUL TOO."

PRAYER

Dear Jesus, I know you see my
wounded heart. I am in the
midst of so much suffering and
hurt. Would you come into my
life and bring healing to those
places? Give me courage to
persevere and hope to see your
hand in my situation, despite
what others think of me. Never
leave me; I need your presence
everyday. I ask you for comfort
in grief, clarity for the future
and strength to follow you. I'm
reaching out to you for a new
freedom in my life. Amen.

Pray this scripture over your own life:
I desire to be your disciple. Show me how to disown my life completely, embrace your cross as my own and surrender to your ways.

Jesus said to all of his followers, "If you truly desire to be my disciple, you must disown your life completely, embrace my 'cross' as your own, and surrender to my ways."

Luke 9:23
(The Passion Translation)

words worth repeating

A CHRISTMAS HEART IS CRUSHED YET COMMITTED, DAMAGED YET DEVOTED.

BECAUSE OF JESUS, WE CAN HOLD BOTH OUR PAIN AND THE PROMISE OF HOPE.

THE PROVISIONS FOR YOUR LIFE FROM THE CROSS ARE ENDLESS.

JESUS WAS PIERCED TO PROVIDE OUR PIERCED HEARTS WITH PURPOSE.

REFLECTION

What hardships has God called you to walk through in your life? Can you name the greatest hardship you have faced? Can you see God's hand in it, and if so, where or how?

Are you willing to trust God even if your heart is pierced? What is currently weighing you down?

How has your reputation been impacted by going all in for Jesus? How is the threat of your reputation keeping you from being all in for Jesus?

How has God brought you comfort or encouragement even in the midst of a wounded season?

AUNT CAROLYN'S BROWNIES

INGREDIENTS

½ cup melted butter
1 cup sugar
1 teaspoon vanilla
2 eggs
½ cup unsifted all purpose flour
½ cup Hershey's Cocoa powder
¼ teaspoon baking powder
¼ teaspoon salt
½ cup chopped nuts (optional)

> Aunt Carolyn is
> Allison's Mom.

DIRECTIONS

Blend melted butter, sugar and vanilla in a mixing bowl. Add eggs; beat well with a spoon. Combine flour, cocoa, baking powder and salt; gradually add to egg mixture until well blended. Stir in nuts. Spread in a greased 9 inch square pan.

Bake at 350 degrees for 25 minutes or until brownies begin to pull away from the edges of the pan. (We like them gooey so 20-25 minutes is enough.) Cool in pan. Frost if desired; cut into squares.

Makes 16 tiny brownies.

START WITH A QUICK
SENTENCE PRAYER

---

*Jesus, I praise you,
glorify you and
rejoice in you.*

Chapter 4

MARY PRAYED AND PRAISED

Have you ever felt overwhelmed and stressed by all the responsibilities during the Christmas season? When my husband, Doyle, accepted his first senior pastor position, I felt the pressure like never before. It was my favorite time of year. I so desperately wanted to have an attitude and outlook like Mary, yet I failed miserably.

Christmas was different and difficult for me as a young pastor's wife. December flew by, leaving me totally exhausted. In addition to decorating my own house, I gathered a team to decorate thousands of square feet at the church. From cooking, baking, shopping and wrapping, everything I did for my own family I also did for my church family. I found myself disappointed that every

BLESSED IS SHE WHO HAS BELIEVED THAT THE LORD WOULD FULFILL HIS PROMISES TO HER!

Luke 1:45

"normal" holiday activity was multiplied for me, and I frequently caved to "bah-humbug syndrome." Even the crisis calls increased because everyone seemed to be running on fumes, both physically and emotionally, during the holiday season. Meanwhile, my extended family who lived 3-7 hours away depending on the side of the family, wanted to know when we would be joining them for their celebrations, adding to the neverending lists of things to do. Eager to hug their sweet necks, I knew that the added effort of packing up a car and driving to be with our families after our church and Christmas morning celebrations would be worth it even if it meant I would be a zombie by the time I arrived.

This is Christmas for a pastor's family.

I remember that first Christmas Eve in Columbus so well because it changed me. The house was prepared with Christmas gifts under the tree, breakfast was ready in the fridge for two excited young boys and the car was packed for our time away with family. We made it to Christmas Eve service to worship with our church. My legs were aching and my toes, which were slightly jammed into black high heels, were throbbing. Yet there I sat with my two precious blond-haired boys by my side, within the gorgeously decorated walls of a church filled with the warm smiles of our church family. As the glow of candlelight and the joy of voices singing *Silent Night* filled the room, my heart began to soften, the physical pain throughout my body began to dissolve, and my soul began to rest. That's when it hit me, it was all worth it.

THERE WAS NO REASON TO BE
OVERWHELMED AS GOD MET ME
THERE ON CHRISTMAS EVE.

My heart aching, I began to pray in a soft whisper, "Thank you, God. You are more than enough for me. You have all of the power, and you deserve all of the glory. You are good. I sing to you! You are worthy, and we celebrate your entrance into the world tonight. My heart is aching, longing to respond to You as Mary did. God, I accept Your responsibilities and plans for my life."

I continued, my prayer gaining strength, "I rely on you, Jesus. Just as Mary continued in her ministry to the very end, so will I. Don't fail me now, Lord. Just as Mary humbled herself, worshipped you and sang for joy, so will I. Just as Mary spent time praying, so will I. Give me peace instead of fear to follow your plans for my life." That moment of reflection and heartfelt prayer became the anthem of my holidays as I adjusted to life with new responsibilities, demands and expectations.

What are you experiencing this holiday season? As December 25th draws closer, how are you feeling? Where is your focus as the season unfolds? If we only give gifts but forget to unwrap the message of Jesus then we've done nothing more than spend money, time and energy, forgetting the promise that Jesus was born to deliver.

IF WE ONLY STAY BUSY AND FORGET
TO UNWRAP THE HOPE OF JESUS,
THEN WE HAVE FORGOTTEN HIM AND
HAVE ONLY EXHAUSTED OURSELVES.

Mary knew the hope that God had filled inside of her. She knew the gravity of the season she was called to embody. When Mary was still pregnant and visited her cousin, Elizabeth, Mary was overcome with joy at the realization of God's call on her life. Mary sang out to God in prayer, praising Him for His goodness. She sang: "My soul glorifies the Lord and my spirit rejoices in God my Savior, for he has been mindful of the humble state of his servant" (Luke 1:46-48). The Passion translation shares her words like this: "My soul is ecstatic, overflowing with praises to God! My spirit bursts with joy over my life-giving God! For he set his tender gaze upon me, his lowly servant girl."

It is normal to experience feelings of being overwhelmed during this demanding season. We juggle so much on behalf of our families, our friends, our neighbors, our churches and our jobs. God calls us to many spaces and to many people, and this season seems especially burdensome. Mary knew this burden, but she kept her gaze centered on Jesus to help her through it. She remained committed to carrying the message and promise of Jesus to others. She praised God through her prayer and her song. She remained devout in her ministry and in prayer. These commitments were central to her Christmas heart. Because Mary's gaze stayed fixed on the gift of Jesus, she reflected His goodness, glory and grace.

What can you let go of this month that though important would allow you to trade your time for resting with Jesus or serving someone who needs Him?

Mary also knew the pain, suffering and disgrace that is a part of life. She was living in a pressure cooker. She faced an unplanned pregnancy, mounting political stress, a great call on her life, a threat to both her life and reputation and much uncertainty about the future - all at a very young age. As life weighed heavily on Mary, something remarkable happened. Instead of rage, bitterness and binging, out of her heart spilled prayer, praise and worship. A Christmas heart knows the pressures of life and still chooses prayer. A Christmas heart acknowledges the pain and still seeks to offer praise.

As Christmas Day fast approaches, your feet are likely tired. Rejoice! You have made it this far. Like Mary, you can stay focused on the true meaning of the season, through worship, prayer and a devotion to His call.

We can rely on His Spirit, His Power and His Word.

Likely the Christmas season will always bring with it more demands and expectations than we can fairly handle. I've learned the art of delegation, the necessity of boundaries and the power of a positive attitude (I've also learned the relief of choosing recipes I can make in advance and simply warm up on Christmas Day, such as one of our favorites: cheese grits). More than anything though, I've learned that a Christmas heart can and will transform those weeks around the holidays. Instead of a zombie with a bah-humbug attitude, I now delight in prioritizing time with Jesus as a critical part of my holiday rhythm. The highlight of my days is sitting in my quiet time chair with my journal and Bible set before me, my coffee in one hand and pen in the other. Some days I have 20 minutes and other days I have two hours, but every minute of time that I spend with God is a gift. From my chair I watch the birds in the snow as the tree lights reflect a warm glow on the glass, and I think of how much He cares for those birds. How much more does He care for me? How much more does He care for you? This practice of being with God has transformed my holiday season more than anything else, and I am confident that the same transformation is available to you.

We serve a very personal God. He is one who draws near, who sees you, who knows you and who loves you so deeply. He inhabits the praises of His people. Our praise is the highest form of prayer. It is our greatest tool in the fight against spiritual warfare. When we worship, pray and praise, the enemy must flee. Take time to sing to Him, praise Him, pray to Him and stay hopeful in Him. He is Emmanuel. He is with you.

Do you believe?

LUKE 1:46-55

AND MARY SAID: "MY SOUL GLORIFIES THE LORD
AND MY SPIRIT REJOICES IN GOD MY SAVIOR,
FOR HE HAS BEEN MINDFUL OF THE HUMBLE
STATE OF HIS SERVANT. FROM NOW ON ALL
GENERATIONS WILL CALL ME BLESSED, FOR THE
MIGHTY ONE HAS DONE GREAT THINGS FOR
ME - HOLY IS HIS NAME. HIS MERCY EXTENDS
TO THOSE WHO FEAR HIM, FROM GENERATION
TO GENERATION. HE HAS PERFORMED MIGHTY
DEEDS WITH HIS ARM; HE HAS SCATTERED THOSE
WHO ARE PROUD IN THEIR INMOST THOUGHTS.
HE HAS BROUGHT DOWN RULERS FROM THEIR
THRONES BUT HAS LIFTED UP THE HUMBLE. HE
HAS FILLED THE HUNGRY WITH GOOD THINGS
BUT HAS SENT THE RICH AWAY EMPTY. HE HAS
HELPED HIS SERVANT ISRAEL, REMEMBERING
TO BE MERCIFUL TO ABRAHAM AND HIS
DESCENDANTS FOREVER, JUST AS HE PROMISED
OUR ANCESTORS."

PRAYER

Dear Jesus, I want to develop a Christmas heart like Mary's. Help me to praise you, sing to you and pray to you. Help me to live out your calling on my life. Even in distress, pain and hardship I want to honor and follow you. I choose to walk forward boldly into the future with you. Show me my assignments in prayer and ministry. Give me active faith to believe you for miracles. I am forever grateful that you would come to rescue me in such a personal way. From the manger to the cross, you are the best Savior I could ever ask for! Happy Birthday Jesus! Amen.

MEMORIZE

"Blessed is she who has believed that the Lord would fulfill his promises to her!"

Luke 1:45

words worth repeating

MY SPIRIT BURSTS WITH JOY OVER
MY LIFE-GIVING GOD!

INSTEAD OF RAGE, BITTERNESS AND
BINGING, OUT OF MARY'S HEART SPILLED
PRAYER, PRAISE AND WORSHIP.

KNOW THE PRESSURE; CHOOSE PRAYER.
ACKNOWLEDGE THE PAIN; SEEK PRAISE.

WE CAN RELY ON HIS SPIRIT,
HIS POWER AND HIS WORD.

EVERY MINUTE OF TIME
THAT I SPEND WITH GOD IS A GIFT.

REFLECTION

What does this season demand of you?
Is all of it necessary? Some activities are
important, good and necessary, but not all.
Finish these statements, and consider how
they might help you to better navigate the
demands of the season:
I must do ...
I would like to ...
I can let go of ...

What emotions are you experiencing
during this demanding season? How
can you recharge in the midst of it all?
Consider these ideas:

- *Kneel by your bed and share your*
  heart with God.
- *Drink extra water with lemon.*
- *Sleep an hour later or go to bed an*
  hour earlier, or go to bed an hour earlier
- *Eat a big salad.*
- *Light a candle, brew some tea and take*
  15 minutes to sit with worship music.
- *Set a specific time to pray about your*
  schedule, the gifts, the family and your
  friends.

What role does worship, song and prayer
have in your Christmas faith journey?

Where do you need to shift your focus
during this season?

CHEESE GRITS

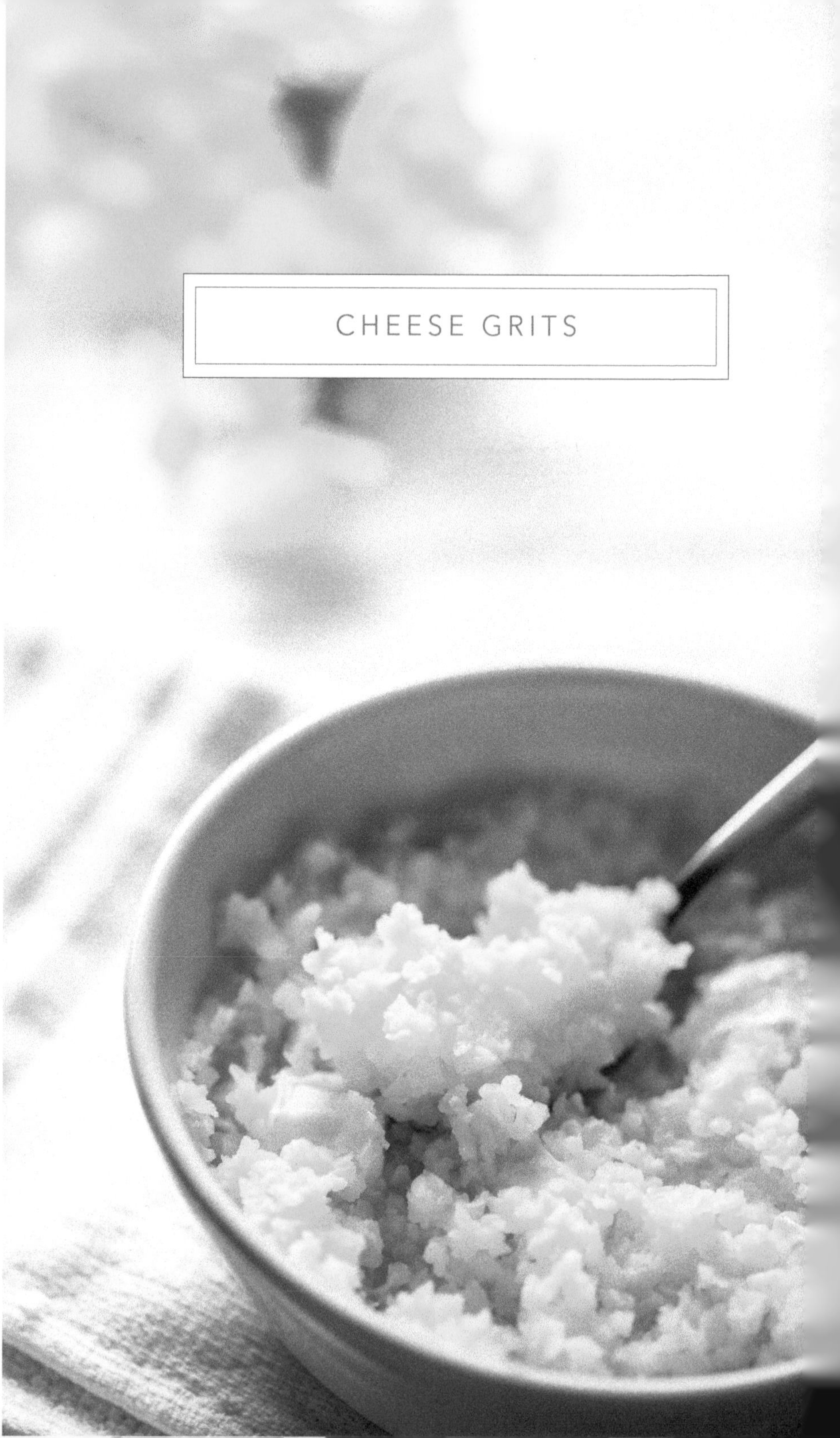

INGREDIENTS

4 cups of boiling water
1 cup instant grits
½ tsp salt
1 stick salted butter
1 cup 2% or whole milk
1 extra large egg
10 ounces grated sharp cheddar cheese

DIRECTIONS

On the stove top, bring water to a boil. Add grits slowly.

Add salt, butter and milk.

Pre whisk your egg and stir in very quickly so it won't cook.

Add cheddar cheese and stir.

Pour into a greased 9x9 glass dish and bake at 350 for 40 minutes.

Serve and eat.

To make ahead, put in refrigerator and bake 40 minutes before serving.

A JACKSON FAMILY TRADITION

These can be made ahead of time and served as a Christmas side dish for breakfast or dinner. These can be doubled to please a large crowd.

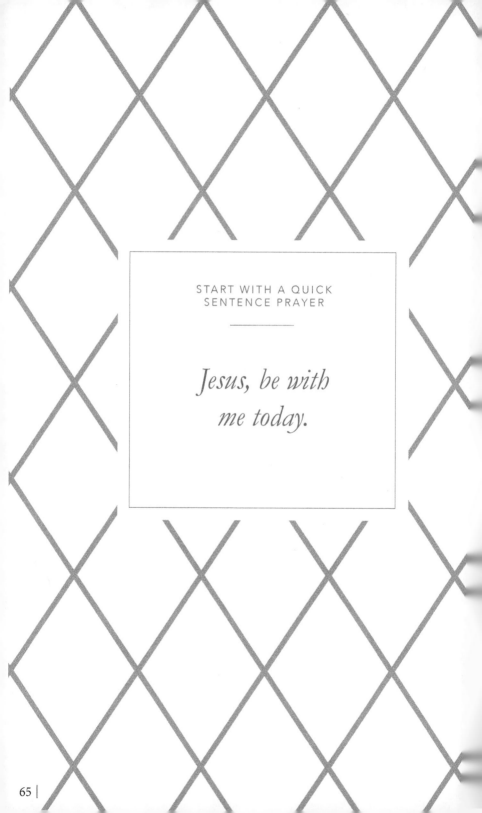

START WITH A QUICK
SENTENCE PRAYER

*Jesus, be with
me today.*

Chapter 5

EMMANUEL: GOD WITH US

It was an unusually warm and balmy Christmas morning in Ohio, but I was snuggled in my flannel Christmas pajamas on the couch, with my reindeer mug and sugar cookie in hand. I was ready to do nothing more than sit, reflect and watch the boys tinker with their new gifts and gadgets. Our dog, Betsy, was practically in my lap as I sat happily content, relishing in the peace of knowing I had finally checked everything off my list before our trip to visit family in Tennessee. I found myself daydreaming about time connecting with our families, the joy of being together, indulging in French Silk Pie and Cranberry Ice. Enjoying this last hour of quiet before we had to pile in the car for our drive, I was jolted from my serenity by my husband abruptly marching through the door. He had been loading up

ALL THIS TOOK PLACE TO FULFILL WHAT THE LORD HAD SAID THROUGH THE PROPHET: "THE VIRGIN WILL CONCEIVE AND GIVE BIRTH TO A SON, AND THEY WILL CALL HIM EMMANUEL" (WHICH MEANS "GOD WITH US").

Matthew 1:22-23

the car for our trip when he rushed into the house announcing, "Hey everybody, we need to cover the swimming pool while it's still warm outside. Let's go. Come on!"

What? Cover the swimming pool on Christmas morning? That wasn't on my list! We had a humongous 40-ft-wide above-ground hand-me-down swimming pool in our backyard; it was a gift from a family who no longer used it. Of course I didn't want the pool to be ruined by leaving it uncovered in the dead of winter, but I certainly wasn't interested in going outside to cover it - not on Christmas Day!

Nonetheless, my husband was determined to cover the pool before we left. With my slippers still on my feet and my mug still in my hand, I moseyed outside to help with the pool covering effort. I was slightly annoyed with the disruption from my contentment, and my husband was slightly annoyed with my lack of enthusiasm and efficiency. I thought to myself, I just want to sit and enjoy Emmanuel - God with us. I just want to savor the sweetness of this Christmas morning and my sugar cookie.

As I attempted to lend a hand (literally a single hand - I was still holding my coffee), my mind began to fill with thoughts about the goodness of Christmas morning, and my heart began to fill with the warming feelings of love toward my boys and my husband. I looked up at the bright

HE IS HERE,
CAME FOR U
HE LOVES U
AND HE LIVI
IN US.

blue sky, and I became overwhelmed. A desire to sing Glory to God came over me. All of this was running through my mind as we stretched the blue plastic cover across the 40-foot pool and tied sand-filled milk jugs around the corners of the cover. That's when it hit me: God IS with us - right there in that moment. There I was in my slippers, holding my Christmas mug, using my one available hand to help tie down the pool cover, and God was with us. I began to laugh out loud with joy welling up in my soul. The boys noticed and asked, "Mom, why are you laughing?" I replied: "Covering this pool is a big task, and we still have to finish packing the car, but it's Christmas and God is with us. My heart is full." The laughter was an outpouring of the joyful gratitude in my heart as I relished in Emmanuel: He is here, He came for us, He loves us and He lives in us.

Merry Christmas! It is a privilege to share with you this journey toward a Christmas heart as we celebrate the birth of our Savior, Jesus Christ. I hope that God has used this time to mold your heart to be more like His. Mother Mary offers us a hopeful example of what a Christmas heart looks like and how a heart for Jesus can carry us through His call on our lives, through our suffering and with our worship.

Mary had a big heart for the scriptures. She knew about the blessings and promise of Abraham. She prayed for the nation of Israel, and she understood the gravity of what God asked of her. She surrendered her fear, and she said yes to God with praise and thanksgiving. Like Mary, we too can surrender to God during this hectic season as we engage a personal relationship with God's son, Jesus. Through that tiny baby born in a manger, we have hope, peace and new life this Christmas and always. Mary was all in for Jesus as she continued to serve through her own suffering and pain. Even in heartache, she embraced joy.

Even in heartache, she embraced joy.

Mary embraced joy because she knew how to enter into God's presence. Through prayer, through worship, through obedience, through suffering, through purity and through song, Mary knew Him, felt Him, saw Him and spoke to Him. That knowing of Emmanuel transcended everything else, and it has the power to transcend everything in our lives as well.

If somebody is missing around the table this year, God is not missing. He's still there. If there is turmoil in your life or relationships, you can still experience peace because of Emmanuel. If you are lonely, overwhelmed, hurting, busy, wondering or waiting, there is peace because Emmanuel.

No matter what, God is with you.

It's not simply the presence of God that sustains us but who God is that provides us with what we need. God is our Counselor, Comforter and Peace. When we need direction, He meets us through prayer and His Word. When we are suffering and in pain, He meets us through His embrace. When we experience angst and turmoil, He steadies us through His perfect peace. No matter the situation, He provides. He is a mighty God.

It's easy to think that bigger presents and better meals and busier schedules will ensure that we experience the best Christmas season, but all of that distracts us from the best the season has to offer: Jesus. We can experience joy in any circumstance so long as we have Jesus.

WE ARE OFFERED PLENTY OF
OPPORTUNITIES TO SEEK JOY AND
PEACE AND COMFORT THROUGH THE
THINGS OF THIS WORLD, BUT IT'S ALL
NOTHING WITHOUT JESUS.

"Peace I leave with you; my peace I give you. I do not give to you as the world gives. Do not let your hearts be troubled and do not be afraid" (John 14:27).

The people walking in darkness have seen a great light; on those living in the land of deep darkness a light has dawned (Isaiah 9:2).

When my boys were young, they would awaken in the middle of the night and cry because of a bad dream. Usually I was sound asleep, but my pastor husband, a light sleeper, quickly met the boys in their room to comfort them and pray with them. He would say, "God is with us, and we can pray and ask for His help. We will tell the bad dreams to go away in Jesus' name." One morning Peter was sitting at the breakfast table, and he announced that he suffered a bad dream the previous night. He added that he prayed on his own and the dream went away. The same Emmanuel who met him when he prayed with his dad also met him personally when he was alone in his room.

Peter learned the power of Emmanuel, and he prayed in faith, "God come now and be with me." Like Peter in the middle of the night, and like Mary throughout her life, we too can pray and ask God to meet us right where we are. I imagine Mary, riding on that donkey toward Bethlehem, her side hurting and her body aching, and I imagine her praying, "Lord I need your help, this seems like a bad dream." She had just birthed the Savior of the world, and the threat to His life was ever increasing. Yet God remained with her, sending her encouragement through the visits from the wise men and the shepherds. She accepted God's plan for her life, and in the midst of her suffering and sorrow, she discovered joy.

Throughout her entire life, Mary demonstrated one thing above all else: faith. She had a lot of faith. It takes faith to experience a Christmas heart. Christmas is about believing. No matter what you are facing this season, you can find Jesus in it. You can discover Emmanuel - God with us, as you treasure and ponder Jesus, as you are available to God's call, as you endure suffering, and as you pray and praise. Through it all, God is with you. I pray you uncover a Christmas heart and discover the greatest gift of all: Jesus. Open up Emmanuel, receive His gift and believe.

Merry Christmas!

ISAIAH 9:6-7

FOR TO US A CHILD IS BORN, TO US A SON IS GIVEN, AND THE GOVERNMENT WILL BE ON HIS SHOULDERS. AND HE WILL BE CALLED WONDERFUL COUNSELOR, MIGHTY GOD, EVERLASTING FATHER, PRINCE OF PEACE. OF THE GREATNESS OF HIS GOVERNMENT AND PEACE THERE WILL BE NO END. HE WILL REIGN ON DAVID'S THRONE AND OVER HIS KINGDOM, ESTABLISHING AND UPHOLDING IT WITH JUSTICE AND RIGHTEOUSNESS FROM THAT TIME ON AND FOREVER. THE ZEAL OF THE LORD ALMIGHTY WILL ACCOMPLISH THIS.

words worth repeating

HE IS HERE,
HE CAME FOR US,
HE LOVES US AND
HE LIVES IN US.

KNOWING EMMANUEL
TRANSCENDS
EVERYTHING ELSE.

GOD IS NOT MISSING.
HE'S STILL THERE.

NO MATTER WHAT,
GOD IS WITH ME.

OH COME, OH COME
EMMANUEL
~ GOD WITH ME.

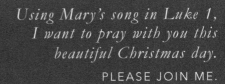

*Using Mary's song in Luke 1,
I want to pray with you this
beautiful Christmas day.*
PLEASE JOIN ME.

PRAYER

Dear Heavenly Father, This morning, we want to say "Glory to You!" We rejoice in you. We thank you for saving us! In our lowly state, you still chose us! Holy God, you have been so good to us. Please extend mercy to our family. May the next generation honor and respect you. We think of all your amazing deeds and how you have pushed away the wicked from our lives. Your strength holds us up. You alone bring down rulers and lift up humble leaders. Please save our nation. We pray that repentance, prayer, holiness and revival would come to every person. Start with us! You alone fill the hungry with good things. We hunger for your Word and thirst for your presence. The riches of this world are empty to me. Keep our eyes away from earthly things. Remember little Israel, and bring her peace and mercy this Christmas morning. We stand today on all the good promises that you gave to Abraham, Israel and to us. Thank you for health, blessing, expansion, freedom, victory and favor. You are faithful always. Merry Christmas, sweet Jesus. Live in our hearts forever. Amen.

REFLECTION

*Who is missing around
your table this Christmas?
What do you miss the most
about them?*

*Describe a time that you
embraced joy in the midst
of sorrow.*

*How has God provided for
you uniquely this year?*

*Write about a time when
you felt God's presence,
Emmanuel, God with you.*

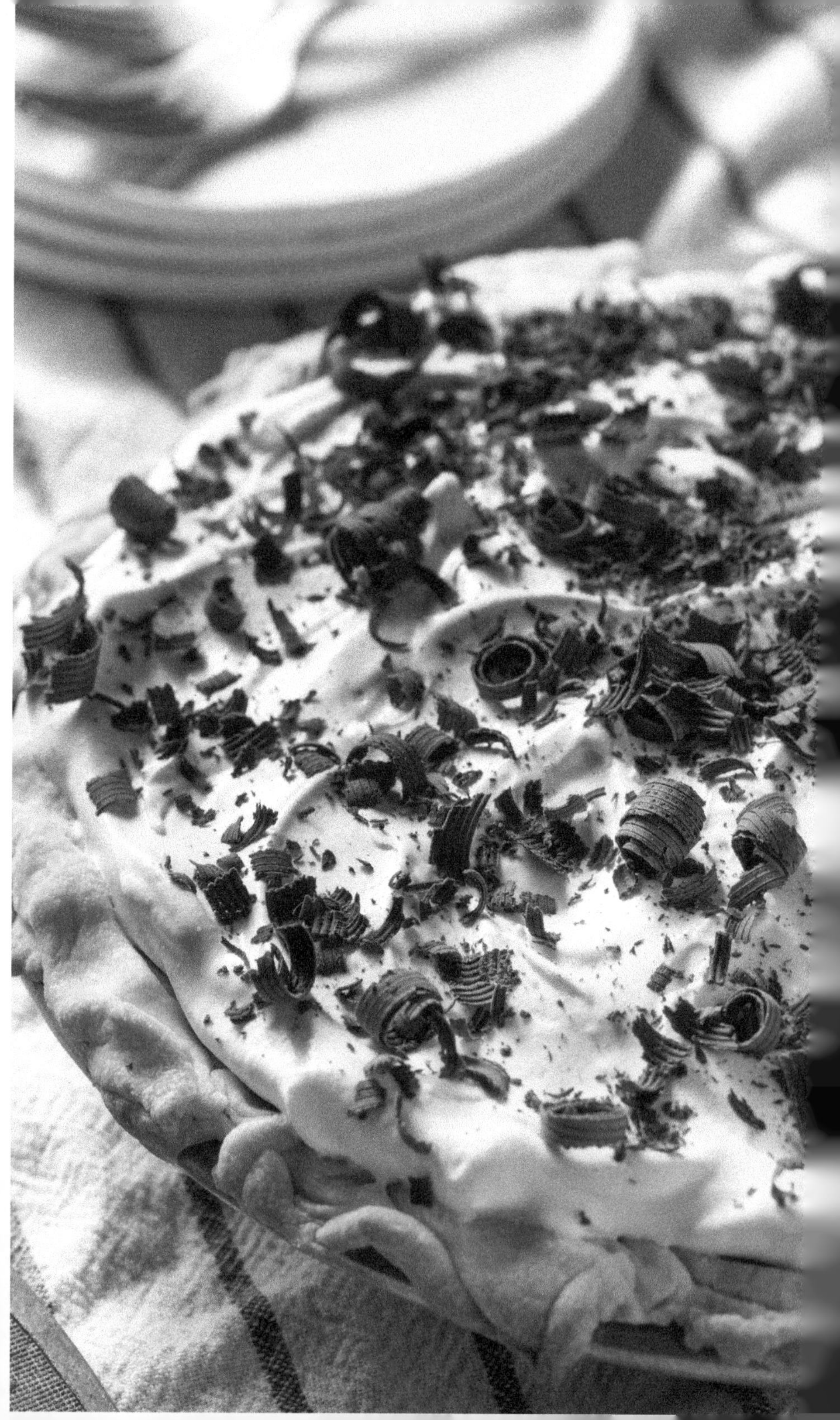

CHOCOLATE FRENCH SILK PIE

INGREDIENTS

1 stick of melted salted butter
3/4 cup sugar
2 squares of unsweetened bakers
    chocolate melted
1 tsp vanilla
2 small eggs
Whipping cream or extra creamy
    Cool Whip
Crushed peppermint

DIRECTIONS

This is a small, simple but delicious pie.
Pre-bake a store bought pie crust, let cool while
doing the following:

In a mixing bowl. Beat butter and sugar until
fluffy. Add melted chocolate, vanilla and 2 small
eggs, one at a time. Beat 5 minutes after adding
each egg. Pour mixture into pie shell, chill.

Add whipped cream and shaved chocolate or
crushed peppermint to the top.

CRANBERRY ICE

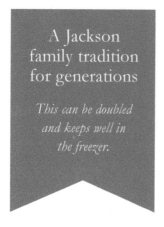

A Jackson
family tradition
for generations

*This can be doubled
and keeps well in
the freezer.*

INGREDIENTS

1 quart or 4 cups of fresh
cranberries
2 tsp Knox Gelatin
2 2/3 cups sugar
1 cup orange juice
(bottled or fresh)
1 large lemon (juiced)

DIRECTIONS

Bring 3 cups water to a boil. Meanwhile wash and drain berries.

Cook berries in boiling water until they soften and begin to slowl
break open. Don't drain the water. Pour the berry and water mixtur
through a sieve to smash the berries and make a paste. Gather this in
large bowl under the sieve. Move quickly to keep it hot. Have all othe
ingredients measured and ready!

Add sugar, stir to dissolve. Add the gelatin, sprinkle and stir to let
dissolve. Add orange and lemon juice. Pour into a non stick bundt pa
and freeze.

Can stir a few times while freezing in the first hour. Any glass dish w
also work, lightly oil with cooking spray. Once fully frozen the next da
set the pan in a tiny bit of hot water to loosen the mold and flip on
a pretty tray. Serve immediately.

CPSIA information can be obtained
at www.ICGtesting.com
Printed in the USA
LVHW071028071220
673527LV00013B/527

9 780578 813349